# SCRIPTURE MEMORY
## MADE EASY

*Scripture Memory Made Easy*
Copyright © 2024 by Rose Publishing

Published by Rose Publishing
An imprint of Tyndale House Ministries
Carol Stream, Illinois
www.hendricksonrose.com

**The *Made Easy* series is a collection of concise, pocket-sized books that summarize key biblical teachings and provide clear, user-friendly explanations to common questions about the Christian faith. Find more *Made Easy* books at www.hendricksonrose.com.**

ISBN 978-1-4964-9021-6

All rights reserved. No part of this work may be reproduced or transmitted in any form or by any means, electronic or mechanical, including photocopying, recording, or by any information storage and retrieval system, without permission in writing from the publisher.

Scripture quotations marked ESV are from The ESV® Bible (The Holy Bible, English Standard Version®), copyright © 2001 by Crossway, a publishing ministry of Good News Publishers. Used by permission. All rights reserved.

Scripture quotations marked NIV are taken from the Holy Bible, *New International Version,*® *NIV.*® Copyright © 1973, 1978, 1984, 2011 by Biblica, Inc.® Used by permission. All rights reserved worldwide.

Scripture quotations marked NKJV are taken from the New King James Version,® copyright © 1982 by Thomas Nelson. Used by permission. All rights reserved.

Scripture quotations marked NLT are taken from the *Holy Bible,* New Living Translation, copyright © 1996, 2004, 2015 by Tyndale House Foundation. Used by permission of Tyndale House Publishers, Carol Stream, Illinois 60188. All rights reserved.

Written by Kalila Herring

Images used under license from Shutterstock.com, except for p. 9: Concord, Wikimedia Commons; p. 11: Wikimedia Commons; p. 77: Jeremy Bishop, Unsplash

Printed by Regent Publishing Services Ltd.
Printed in China
May 2024, 1st printing

# CONTENTS

Introduction ............................................................ 5

Ten Benefits of Scripture Memory ..................................... 17

Getting Started ....................................................... 29

Twenty Memorization Strategies ....................................... 49

Scriptures to Memorize ............................................... 75

Resources ............................................................. 91

Notes ................................................................. 95

*I will study your commandments and reflect on your ways. I will delight in your decrees and not forget your word.*

PSALM 119:15–16 NLT

# INTRODUCTION

*Jesus replied, "You must love the L*ORD *your God with all your heart, all your soul, and all your mind." This is the first and greatest commandment. A second is equally important: "Love your neighbor as yourself." The entire law and all the demands of the prophets are based on these two commandments.*

MATTHEW 22:37–40 NLT

*[Jesus said,] "If you love me, you will keep my commandments."*

JOHN 14:15 ESV

Are you ready to explore the exciting adventure of Scripture memory? You have made an important step in drawing closer to the Lord! The first Scripture passage above teaches that the most important command in the Bible is to love God. The second passage, from the Gospel of John, shows us *how* we are to love God: by keeping the commandments in his Word.

To do this, we need to know those commandments and keep them front and center in our minds and hearts. Then we must commit them to memory so we can quickly determine how to think and act in every situation. This is especially important for parents and mentors. They must "let the word of Christ dwell in [them] richly" (Col. 3:16 NKJV) to set a good example and effectively teach God's Word.

The practice of memorizing God's Word has plenty of support in Scripture. Yet many people struggle to understand its importance and actually do it. When Bible verses can be pulled up on a smartphone in a matter of seconds, Scripture memory doesn't seem to matter that much. Sadly, the result is that Scripture memory is not built into society and churches the way it once was in the past. Here are a few reasons the Bible offers for why we should be intentional about committing God's Word to memory:

> *"These words which I command you today shall be in your heart. You shall teach them diligently to your children, and shall talk of them when you sit in your house, when you walk by the way, when you lie down, and when you rise up."* (Deut. 6:5–7 NKJV)

> *"Commit yourselves wholeheartedly to these words of mine. Tie them to your hands and wear them on your forehead as reminders."* (Deut. 11:18 NLT)

> *"I have stored up your word in my heart, that I might not sin against you."* (Ps. 119:11 ESV)

## Always Ready

"Storing up" God's Word in our hearts, "tying" his commands to our hands, and "wearing them" on our foreheads—each of these phrases means that we know and recall Scripture well. The Holy Spirit, who lives inside those who have placed their faith in Jesus, will also help us recall Scripture that we have read and memorized:

> *Jesus stood up and cried out …*
> *"Whoever believes in me, as the Scripture has said,*
> *'Out of his heart will flow rivers of living water.'"*
> *Now this he said about the Spirit, whom those*
> *who believed in him were to receive.*
>
> JOHN 7:37–39 ESV

> *When He, the Spirit of truth, has come,*
> *He will guide you into all truth.*
>
> JOHN 16:13 NKJV

The Holy Spirit uses memorized Scripture to help us remember the hope we have in the Lord, as well as his life-giving instructions. Then we have God's encouragement and guidance for whatever situation we face, even at a moment's notice. These Scriptures remind us that God and his Word can strengthen us in every type of circumstance:

### 1. In times of temptation

*"God is faithful; he will not let you be tempted beyond what you can bear. But when you are tempted, he will also provide a way out so that you can endure it."* (1 Cor. 10:13 ESV)

*"The word of God is alive and powerful. It is sharper than the sharpest two-edged sword, cutting between soul and spirit, between joint and marrow. It exposes our innermost thoughts and desires."* (Heb. 4:12 NLT)

### 2. In times of trouble

*"The Lord is my light and my salvation—whom shall I fear?"* (Ps. 27:1 ESV)

*"God is our refuge and strength, a very present help in trouble."* (Ps. 46:1 NKJV)

### 3. In our everyday routine as we draw near to the Lord

*"Search for the Lord and for his strength; continually seek him."* (1 Chron. 16:11 NLT)

*"Draw near to God and He will draw near to you."* (James 4:8 NKJV)

# A Little History

Did you know that the practice of memorization is an ancient discipline? Stories, poems, and history were passed down from speaker to speaker. In the same way, stories and truths in Scripture were communicated orally from the very beginning. Here are some examples:[1]

### 1. When Moses received God's Law at Mount Sinai

*"[Moses] called together the elders of the people and told them everything the LORD had commanded him."* (Ex. 19:7 NLT)

### 2. Before the Israelites entered the Promised Land

*"Forty years after the Israelites left Egypt, ... Moses addressed the people of Israel, telling them everything the LORD had commanded him to say."* (Deut. 1:3 NLT)

### 3. After the Israelites entered the Promised Land

*"[Joshua] read all the words of the law, the blessing and the curse, according to all that is written in the Book of the Law. There was not a word of all that Moses commanded that Joshua did not read before all the assembly of Israel, and the women, and the little ones, and the sojourners who lived among them."* (Josh. 8:34–35 ESV)

Leaf from Papyrus Bodmer XXIV

### 4. When King Josiah found the lost Scriptures in the temple

*"The king went up to the house of the Lord with all the men of Judah ... and all the people, both small and great. And he read in their hearing all the words of the Book of the Covenant."* (2 Kings 23:2 NKJV)

### 5. When God's people returned from a long exile in a foreign land

*"Ezra the priest brought the Book of the Law before the assembly ... and read aloud to everyone who could understand. All the people listened closely to the Book of the Law."* (Neh. 8:2–3 NLT)

### 6. When Jesus spoke at his hometown synagogue

*"He came to Nazareth, where He had been brought up. And as His custom was, He went into the synagogue on the Sabbath day, and stood up to read. And He was handed the book of the prophet Isaiah."* (Luke 4:16–17 NKJV)

### 7. In the early church

*"Focus on reading the Scriptures to the church, encouraging the believers, and teaching them."* (1 Tim. 4:13 NLT)

In Bible times, the ease and abundance of paper, pens, and books did not exist, so the Scriptures were written on stone, papyrus, and animal skins. These rare copies were kept in the temple, in synagogues, and in private homes where church gatherings were held. Congregations had access to the copies only when they came together and listened as the Word of God was read aloud. The people would then memorize the Scriptures by listening carefully.

In the Middle Ages, monks, nuns, and other church leaders were required to memorize all 150 psalms. Handwritten books called "illuminated manuscripts" helped medieval Christians become dedicated memorizers. These beautiful, artistic presentations of Scripture were written on parchment (animal skins) and decorated with painted illustrations and precious metals. The decorations were prompts that helped readers recall the text.[2] Throughout the ages, a focus on memorization has continued:

- The famous reformer Martin Luther "ran through the Scriptures from memory."[3]

- Missionary martyr Jim Elliot memorized Scripture in the cafeteria line.[4]

- Author Laura Ingalls Wilder memorized Scripture in her prairie home.[5]

Perhaps the best example of Scripture memorization, however, comes from Jesus himself. He fully embodied the Scriptures, living a perfect life as fully God and fully human. Let's take a look.

Bible of Matteo di Planisio (illuminated manuscript)

# Jesus as "the Word"

> *In the beginning was the Word, and the Word was with God, and the Word was God.*
>
> JOHN 1:1 ESV

---

The apostle John referred to Jesus as "the Word" and said, "The Word became human and made his home among us" (John 1:14 NLT). Jesus is the living Word of God. It's no wonder that he frequently spoke Scripture from memory during his ministry on earth. Jesus used memorized Scripture to help others understand who he was and what God's will really looks like. He quoted many times from what we now call the Old Testament:

## 1. Jesus responded with Scripture when Satan tempted him in the desert.

*"It is written, 'Man shall not live by bread alone, but by every word that proceeds from the mouth of God.'"* (Matt. 4:4 NKJV, quoting Deut. 8:3)

*"It is written again, 'You shall not tempt the Lord your God.'"* (Matt. 4:7 NKJV, quoting Deut. 6:16)

*"Away with you, Satan! For it is written, 'You shall worship the Lord your God, and Him only you shall serve.'"* (Matt. 4:10 NKJV, quoting Deut. 6:13)

## 2. Jesus quoted from Scripture in many of his teachings, including the Sermon on the Mount.

*"You have heard that our ancestors were told, 'You must not murder. If you commit murder, you are subject to judgment.'"* (Matt. 5:21 NLT, quoting Ex. 20:13; Deut. 5:17)

*"You have heard the commandment that says, 'You must not commit adultery.'"* (Matt. 5:27 NLT, quoting Ex. 20:14; Deut. 5:18)

*"You have also heard that our ancestors were told, 'You must not break your vows; you must carry out the vows you make to the LORD.'"* (Matt. 5:33 NLT, quoting Num. 30:2)

## 3. Jesus referenced passages from the Psalms and the book of Daniel when he was questioned by the high priest at his trial.

*"I tell you, from now on you will see the Son of Man seated at the right hand of Power and coming on the clouds of heaven."* (Matt. 26:64 ESV, quoting Ps. 110:1 and Dan. 7:13)

## 4. Even as he was dying on the cross, Jesus spoke words from Scripture.

*"Jesus cried out with a loud voice, saying, … 'My God, my God, why have you forsaken me?'"* (Matt. 27:46 ESV, quoting Ps. 22:1)

## All the Right Reasons

Like all spiritual practices, memorization should start with the heart instead of a desire to "earn points" with God. We don't want to be like the Pharisees of Jesus's day. They acted religiously and prayed long prayers, yet Jesus said they were "like whitewashed tombs, which outwardly appear beautiful, but within are full of dead people's bones and all uncleanness." (Matt. 23:27 ESV). Clearly their hearts weren't in the right place! We see an emphasis on the importance of the heart throughout the Bible:

*"When you pray, don't be like the hypocrites who love to pray publicly on street corners and in the synagogues where everyone can see them. I tell you the truth, that is all the reward they will ever get. But when you pray, go away by yourself, shut the door behind you, and pray to your Father in private."* (Matt. 6:5–6 NLT)

*"When you fast, comb your hair and wash your face. Then no one will notice that you are fasting, except your Father, who knows what you do in private."* (Matt. 6:17–18 NLT)

*"If I speak in the tongues of men and of angels, but have not love, I am a noisy gong or a clanging cymbal. And if I have prophetic powers, and understand all mysteries and all*

# INTRODUCTION

*knowledge, and if I have all faith, so as to remove mountains, but have not love, I am nothing."* (1 Cor. 13:1-2 ESV)

Just as we receive no spiritual benefit from fasting to be seen or praying to be heard in public, memorization to merely store information or show off to others profits us nothing. Memorization means something only when we use it in concert with prayer, worship, and a heart that desires to better know the Lord. If we memorize to win a contest, the prize is the reward. But if we memorize to better align our desires with God's will for our lives, we are blessed with knowledge and wisdom for a lifetime. Psalm 1:1-2 describes how these blessings work:

*"Oh, the joys of those who do not follow the advice of the wicked, or stand around with sinners, or join in with mockers. But they delight in the law of the Lord, meditating on it day and night."* (NLT)

We can find *delight* in the Scriptures as we think about them. Doing so helps us adjust our actions to reflect what we have learned. All the while, we are filled with thankfulness and joy because we are drawing near to God and turning away from evil. And this is just the beginning. Next, we'll take a look at even more ways that memorizing Scripture can help us in our Christian walk.

*I know of no other single practice in the Christian life more rewarding, practically speaking, than memorizing Scripture.... No other single exercise pays greater spiritual dividends!*

CHARLES SWINDOLL,
*Growing Strong in the Seasons of Life*

# TEN BENEFITS OF SCRIPTURE MEMORY

## 1. We understand God's desires.

*Don't copy the behavior and customs of this world, but let God transform you into a new person by changing the way you think. Then you will learn to know God's will for you, which is good and pleasing and perfect.*

ROMANS 12:2 NLT

Romans 12:2 tells us that when we change our thoughts to align with God's Word, we will become more like Christ. That means the more we meditate on Scripture, the easier it will be to train our minds and souls to live according to God's desires. Just as a painter needs to continually look at a subject in order to replicate its image on canvas, we need to continually look to Jesus, who is revealed through the Scriptures. But unlike visual art, the written Word can be memorized and brought to mind whenever it is needed! Because the Holy Spirit dwells in us, "we have the mind of Christ" (1 Cor. 2:16 ESV), and he helps us to recall what we've learned and read. "The Lord—who is the Spirit—makes us more and more like him as we are changed into his glorious image" (2 Cor. 3:18 NLT)

## 2. We resist sin and Satan.

*Take up the whole armor of God, that you may be able to withstand in the evil day, and having done all, to stand firm. Stand therefore, having fastened on the belt of truth, and having put on the breastplate of righteousness, and, as shoes for your feet, having put on the readiness given by the gospel of peace. In all circumstances take up the shield of faith, with which you can extinguish all the flaming darts of the evil one; and take the helmet of salvation, and the sword of the Spirit, which is the word of God.*

EPHESIANS 6:13–17 ESV

An ancient warrior's uniform included many different pieces. Most were used for defense against an enemy's attack: a breastplate, a shield, a helmet, sturdy shoes. But a soldier's *sword* helped with both defense and offense. In spiritual terms, the Holy Spirit uses Scripture as a "sword" to prevent the enemy's fiery darts from finding their mark. Scripture can destroy Satan's darts when he attacks with anything from temptation to anxiety to discouragement—every kind of thought and feeling that isn't from God. And just as a soldier would never leave his weapon at home, so we should always be armed with God's Word.

When our patience is being tested, we often wish we could naturally have self-control. But so many times, our reactions reflect old patterns of instant, angry responses. We all have moments when acting out in sin is easy to do. Our reactions can be triggered by something as trivial as hunger pangs, a traffic delay, a coworker's mistake, or discovering we left the ice cream in the trunk of the car. It takes intentional work to imitate Christ in these situations. Proverbs 7:1–3 talks about how a son is to go about keeping his father's commands, and the same principle applies to us as we seek to obey our Father God's commands:

> *"My son, keep my words, and treasure my commands within you. Keep my commands and live, and my law as the apple of your eye. Bind them on your fingers; write them on the tablet of your heart."* (NKJV)

Once again, the Bible illustrates how we must fill our hearts and minds with God's Word so that it influences our thoughts, words, and actions. Proverbs 7 also describes the opposite scenario: a foolish young man suffers the consequences of not following God's ways. When he allowed a married woman to seduce him, "he did not know it would cost his life" (v. 23). This young man would not have gone "to the chambers of death" (v. 27) if he had treasured God's commandments, keeping them as the "apple" of his eye and writing them on the "tablet" of his heart.

Interestingly, Psalm 119:9–11 portrays a sharp contrast between the foolish young man of Proverbs 7 and a young man who is wise. The key difference is that the wise man remembers God's Word and acts upon it:

> *"How can a young man keep his way pure? By guarding it according to your word.... I have stored up your word in my heart, that I might not sin against you."* (ESV)

Whether we're fighting a battle against a specific sin or the many temptations that pop up every day, this passage in Psalm 119 offers a clear path to resisting Satan and keeping our way pure. We must intentionally guard our hands, hearts, eyes, ears, and mouths. James 1:14–15 says, "Temptation comes from our own desires, which entice us and drag us away. These desires give birth to sinful actions. And when sin is allowed to grow, it gives birth to death" (NLT). When we memorize Scripture, we are better equipped to obey God's commands and live well.

## 3. We find hope amid suffering.

*Such things were written in the Scriptures long ago to teach us. And the Scriptures give us hope and encouragement as we wait patiently for God's promises to be fulfilled.*

ROMANS 15:4 NLT

---

Sin is not the only struggle we face. Much suffering comes from simply living in this fallen world. And when long, difficult trials come, the pain can be enough to dull our hearts and minds to anything but the throb. During these times, we often don't have enough energy to be intentional about reading the Bible. We simply live in survival mode, taking one moment at a time.

Yet one of the amazing things about memorizing Scripture is that when we're going through difficulties, those words of hope we have stored away often surface again. Holding on to them can keep us afloat when we feel like we're drowning. Even repeating the same verse over and over can help us get through a panic attack or the shock of bad news. Recalling God's promises brings safety as the ground seems to fall away beneath our feet. They remind us that as God's children, his love and provision are eternal, no matter what may try to harm us. The result is summed up in 2 Corinthians 4:16–18:

*"Though our outer self is wasting away, our inner self is being renewed day by day. For this light momentary*

*affliction is preparing for us an eternal weight of glory beyond all comparison, as we look not to the things that are seen but to the things that are unseen. For the things that are seen are transient, but the things that are unseen are eternal."* (ESV)

## 4. We encourage others.

*Encourage each other and build each other up.*

1 THESSALONIANS 5:11 NLT

Even when we are not facing temptations, trials, and suffering, we know friends and fellow church members who are. Often we can encourage them with a simple acknowledgment of grief or a whisper that we are praying

for them. Sometimes, however, it is appropriate to share Scriptures that will bring hope and relief. When writing a card, it's easy to look up verses to include. But when we're physically present with someone, it's ideal to share comforting Scriptures without the awkwardness of searching for an appropriate passage. Proverbs 25:11 says, "Timely advice is lovely, like golden apples in a silver basket." (NLT). Being able to speak the right verse that truly lifts up the downtrodden is an art form indeed.

## 5. We worship.

> *I will study your commandments and reflect on your ways. I will delight in your decrees and not forget your word.*
>
> PSALM 119:15–16 NLT

As already mentioned, the primary purpose of Scripture memory is to draw near to the Lord. The same is true of Bible study, church attendance, and prayer. We memorize as an act of worship, praising God for the good things and praying for help with the hard things. It allows us to say "Bless the Lord, O my soul" throughout the day as we align ourselves with his revealed will (Ps. 103:1 ESV).

Adding Scripture memory to our regular time with the Lord might seem difficult because we aren't used to the discipline that memorization requires. Reading the Bible or a devotional book or spending a few minutes in prayer are not hard in comparison! Like fasting, Scripture memorization requires mental and physical work. The payoff, however, is that Scripture memorization will add rich layers to our devotional life.

Puritan pastor Thomas Watson said that "the reason we come away so cold from reading [the Bible] is, because we do not warm ourselves at the fires of meditation."[6] Memorization helps with this element of meditation. In turn, our prayer times and Bible reading are much sweeter!

This enhances our worship and creates a lifelong habit of staying in Scripture.

## 6. We better understand the Bible.

*Be a good worker, one who does not need to be ashamed and who correctly explains the word of truth.*

2 TIMOTHY 2:15 NLT

Scripture memory will help us to better understand the Bible, but only if we keep memorized passages within the full context of God's Word. Including Scripture memory as part of regular Bible study and devotions can help us accomplish that goal. Then we are also less likely to use memorized Scripture as "magic words" to apply to any situation. We must never recite Scripture like an incantation! God's Word is indeed "living and powerful" (Heb. 4:12 NKJV), but memorizing it to secure the outcome we would like is not the correct motivation.

It's true there will always be seasons when we find ourselves needing to focus on certain sections of the Bible, such as the Psalms. But a broad reading of Scripture will

help us understand how memorized passages fit into God's entire revealed story. Can we memorize passages from Romans or James without engaging with the Old Testament? Of course, but our understanding will be much richer if we have done so. Or flip that around: When reading the Old Testament, we might come across a verse we recall is quoted in the New Testament. All of this is especially helpful if we're teaching the Bible. The better our understanding of the big picture, the more likely we will brainstorm creative ways of presenting lessons. We'll also easily draw upon what we know and avoid losing time looking everything up.

## 7. We pray.

*Always be joyful. Never stop praying.*

1 THESSALONIANS 5:16–17 NLT

---

When we just don't have the right words to pray, the Holy Spirit helps us by praying for us (Rom. 8:26–27). But sometimes he helps us by bringing memorized Scripture to our minds. These words can be turned into prayers that reflect the actual, true promises of God. Praying the Scriptures is a powerful way to pray according to God's will. It also helps assure us of God's love, care, and affection in all circumstances. Many of the psalms, for example, can guide our prayers in times of trial, repentance, thanksgiving, uncertainty, and joy.

## 8. We share the gospel.

*Go and make disciples of all the nations, baptizing them in the name of the Father and the Son and the Holy Spirit. Teach these new disciples to obey all the commands I have given you.*

MATTHEW 28:19–20 NLT

Sharing the gospel is part of the call of every Christian. The apostle Peter said, "If someone asks about your hope as a believer, always be ready to explain it." (1 Peter 3:15 NLT). And as the apostle Paul says in the book of Romans, how can people believe in Christ if they haven't heard about him? All believers have the opportunity to tell others about Jesus as they go about their daily lives. Quoting memorized Scripture is part of being ready with an explanation of what Christ has done for us.

Consider Acts 8:26–40: When an angel commanded Philip to travel to the south, Philip used Scripture to share the gospel with an important Ethiopian official along the way. The official eagerly believed and asked to be baptized. Another example is when the apostle Paul wrote to Timothy and reminded him that as a pastor, he needed to be ready to share the gospel "whether the time is favorable or not," whatever the situation (2 Tim. 4:2 NLT). The same is true for us, for we can never know in advance what opportunities to share the good news might present themselves.

## 9. We equip children.

*Direct your children onto the right path,*
*and when they are older, they will not leave it.*

PROVERBS 22:6 NLT

In order for children to truly thrive and grow in biblical faith, they need more than a prayer and Bible story before bed and church classes on the weekend. As we've seen from Deuteronomy 6:5–7, parents are to diligently teach the Word of God throughout the day. Children are always watching and listening, so they quickly mimic the attitudes, words, and actions they observe. As parents memorize, recite, and apply Scripture in their lives, children will have an example for doing the same. This will especially help them as they grow older and need to own their faith.

Kids can practice memorization during a scheduled, set-apart time or as part of personal devotions. Another opportunity is during family devotions, when everyone is memorizing the same full or partial verse. In a homeschool setting, memorization can easily be worked into the daily Bible lesson (for more about the previous two options, see the heading "Choosing Your Team" in the next chapter). Whether you're a parent, family member, friend, or volunteer at children's church, Vacation Bible School, or Awana, your role matters! Modeling memorization to little ones will help them recall God's Word and apply it.

## 10. We improve our thinking skills.

> *We destroy arguments and every lofty opinion*
> *raised against the knowledge of God,*
> *and take every thought captive to obey Christ.*
>
> 2 CORINTHIANS 10:5 ESV

Let's go back to the argument that says "We have smartphones now—with *searchable* Bibles—so why memorize if we can find the perfect verse in seconds?" As it turns out, memorization helps the brain in unique ways that simply reading will never duplicate. It builds pathways in our brains that can help improve overall memory. It frees us to focus on new things since we already have so many core concepts down pat. There is also evidence that memorization helps critical-thinking skills. As we store God's Word in our hearts and minds, we won't have to hem and haw over what course of action to choose. Instead, we'll act on verses that direct our feet toward righteousness.

# GETTING STARTED

## Choosing a Translation

Deciding which translation to use for memorization is an easy decision for those who are partial to a particular Bible version. Or if you're memorizing with your church, your decision might default to the specific translation your church uses so that there is continuity in preaching, reading, and study. Many of us, however, have used a wide variety of translations throughout our lives, depending on our needs and interests at the time. This book quotes a variety of translations, often depending on which one is most understandable. For family Bible study and memorization, adults may prefer one translation for its accuracy or turn of phrase and opt for a more understandable version for the children.  To sort through some options, take a look at the following chart. It presents several of the most popular English translations of the Bible available today.

| TRANSLATION | YEAR* | DESCRIPTION |
|---|---|---|
| King James Version (KJV) | 1611, 1769 | Used by adults who prefer the English found in older versions. |
| American Standard Version (ASV) | 1901 | Very formal. Used for serious Bible study. |
| Revised Standard Version (RSV) | 1952, 1971 | Based on the ASV |
| Amplified Bible (AMP) | 1965, 2015 | Uses a unique system of punctuation, typefaces, and synonyms (in parentheses) to more fully explain words. |
| Revised New Jerusalem Bible (RNJB) | 1966, 1985, 2019 | Typically used by Roman Catholics for serious Bible study. Includes the Apocrypha. |
| New American Bible, Revised Edition (NABRE) | 1970, 1986, 2011 | Widely used by Roman Catholics of all ages. Includes the Apocrypha. |
| New American Standard Bible (NASB) | 1971, 1995, 2020 | Used by adults for serious Bible study. |
| Good News Translation (GNT) | 1976, 1992 | Used by children and believers for whom English is not their first language. |
| New International Version (NIV) | 1978, 1984, 2011 | Modern translation aimed to be acceptable to many denominations. Currently the best-selling Bible version. |

**GETTING STARTED**

| TRANSLATION | YEAR* | DESCRIPTION |
|---|---|---|
| New King James Version (NKJV) | 1982 | Modern language translation to maintain the structure and beauty of the KJV. |
| New Century Version (NCV) | 1987, 1991 | Uses footnotes to clarify ancient customs. Used by children and teenagers for personal devotional reading. |
| New Revised Standard Version Updated Edition (NRSVue) | 1989, 2021 | Historically ecumenical in its reception, being accepted by Episcopal, Presbyterian, and US Catholic Bishops. |
| Contemporary English Version (CEV) | 1995 | Recommended for children and people who do not speak English as their first language. |
| God's Word Translation (GW) | 1995 | Translated by a committee of biblical scholars and English reviewers to ensure accurate, natural English. |
| New International Reader's Version (NIrV) | 1996, 1998, 2014 | Simple words and short sentences to appeal to a lower reading level. |
| New Living Translation (NLT) | 1996, 2004, 2015 | Easy-to-read modern version. |

| TRANSLATION | YEAR* | DESCRIPTION |
|---|---|---|
| English Standard Version (ESV) | 2001 | Derived from the RSV. Used by teenagers and adults for serious Bible study. |
| The Message (MSG) | 2002, 2018 | Re-creates the common language in which the Bible was written into today's common language. |
| Christian Standard Bible (CSB) | 2004, 2017 | Used by teenagers and adults for personal devotions and Bible study. Revision of the Holman Christian Standard Bible (HCSB). |
| Common English Bible (CEB) | 2011 | Diverse team of translators from 22 faith traditions in American, African, Asian, European, and Latino communities. |

*Year complete Bible translation was released and later revisions

## Choosing What to Memorize

Once you set your mind on memorizing Scripture, the next question is, *Memorize what?* With so many excellent options, it can be hard to choose. You need to focus on topics that will keep you learning for the long haul. One suggestion is to start with the passages listed in the chapter "Scriptures to Memorize." Another is to adopt one or more of the following approaches:

### Life Verses

Are there specific passages that have spoken strongly to you throughout your Christian walk? Such passages are often called "life verses." They might overlap with many commonly suggested verses for memorization, or they may not. If you haven't already started a list of key life verses, now is a great time to start. Think about Scriptures you would mention when telling others how God is working in your life. Which verses help you understand the importance of having a right relationship with God? Which passages illustrate how he has encouraged you along the way?

*My life verses are:*

_____

_____

_____

# Most Popular Life Verses

**FROM BIBLE GATEWAY**

1. "For God so loved the world that he gave his one and only Son, that whoever believes in him shall not perish but have eternal life." (John 3:16 NIV)

2. "'For I know the plans I have for you,' declares the Lord, 'plans to prosper you and not to harm you, plans to give you hope and a future.'" (Jer. 29:11 NIV)

3. "And we know that in all things God works for the good of those who love him, who have been called according to his purpose." (Rom. 8:28 NIV)

4. "Even though I walk through the darkest valley, I will fear no evil, for you are with me; your rod and your staff, they comfort me." (Ps. 23:4 NIV)

5. "Surely your goodness and love will follow me all the days of my life, and I will dwell in the house of the Lord forever." (Ps. 23:6 NIV)[7]

## GETTING STARTED

### *Entire Chapters*

If you have already memorized one or two verses—or simply like diving into new projects—then memorizing a whole chapter is a sensible next step. Skimming through the book of Psalms is often a good starting point, since many have a familiar structure. Memorizing an entire chapter or psalm is sometimes easier and more rewarding than tackling single, disconnected verses. In the big picture of an entire chapter, one verse flows into the next. There is also a logical order for each sentence, helping your mind stay on task.

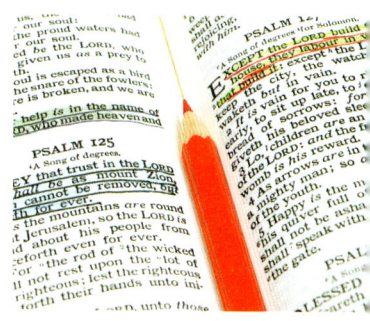

If you decide to go this route, make sure you thoroughly read the chapter or the psalm first. You're more likely to stick to your plan if the content is appealing on a deep level. Remember that you will be reading and reciting this topic day after day, week after week.

*Some of my favorite Bible passages or psalms are:*

_____

_____

_____

## *Entire Books*

If you are ready for an even bigger challenge, consider memorizing an entire book of the Bible. For many people, this is a natural next step if they've chosen to start with the first chapter of a book. And if jumping around is more your style, that's fine too! But how in the world is memorizing an entire book even feasible? Many of the most successful

Scripture memorizers, such as Tom Meyer, "The Bible Memory Man," divide each verse into separate lines and then count the number of words in each line. This number then acts as a memory aid as they memorize the passage. This option for memorizing Scripture also provides an opportunity to study the Bible in depth. You might find yourself using commentaries and other resources that help you move beyond the basic meaning of the passage.

*Books of the Bible I'd consider memorizing are:*

---

---

---

## *The Navigators' Topical Memory System*

If you thrive more on following a plan that has already been mapped out, you might be interested in trying the Navigators' Topical Memory System. Sections such as "Live the New Life," "Proclaim Christ," and "Grow in Christlikeness" include subtopics, each with two memory passages. The system includes the time-honored tool of flash cards, as well as a workbook with a helpful weekly schedule for memorizing each verse. This program is very helpful for people in the following groups:

- Young Christians
- People who are new to memorization
- People with busy schedules
- Anyone who isn't comfortable creating their own program

*Topics I would like to memorize include:*

_____

_____

_____

_____

## Choosing Your Team

Memorizing solo may not appeal to everyone. If you or others in your family fit into this category, perhaps you will find an opportunity to work on memorization within a group setting. Let's look at some of the most common.

### Church

Memorization as a church sends a clear message that Scripture memory is an important practice in today's world. Many churches have built-in opportunities for Scripture memory during the service, such as reciting the Lord's Prayer or the Apostle's Creed. A memory passage can also be included as a separate part of the service, perhaps with the verses printed in the bulletin or displayed on a screen. Throughout the week, the passage can be included in church newsletters or posted on social media accounts. The benefits of a congregation-wide memorization effort are many:

- Unity is built as members learn the same biblical principles (Eph. 4:11–13).

- Connections are fostered as mature Christians find joy in helping newer Christians.

- Church members who might not consider memorizing on their own are encouraged to join the group effort.

- Families have opportunities to discuss God's Word.

# Fighter Verses

Pastor John Piper and Bethlehem Baptist Church memorized "fighter" verses to help them resist temptation, as Jesus did in the wilderness. As they began, Piper encouraged them with these words:

*You may doubt that you can do this, especially if you are older. But ask yourself this question: If I offered you $1,000 for every verse you memorized in the next week, how many do you think you could memorize? Yet God says of his word[s] in Psalm 19:10–11, "They are more desirable than gold, yes, than much fine gold; sweeter also than honey and the drippings of the honeycomb. Moreover, by them thy servant is warned; in keeping them there is great reward." The real value of the word is far greater than $1,000 a verse. The question is this: Do you believe it? Believing this will be the crucial motivation you need.[8]*

## *Discipleship Groups and Mentoring*

As an alternative (or in addition) to a church-wide focus, memorization in small groups or church classes can also work quite well. If a small group is studying a book of the Bible, memorization exercises can naturally be included. Even book studies have themes with scriptural applications to key verses. In small groups, there is more opportunity for actual practice. Attendees can take turns reciting and checking verses, as well as explaining how the assigned passage relates to their faith testimony. Another idea is for class members to share how the passage has impacted their actions and thoughts throughout the week (this can also be a great icebreaker at the beginning of class).

In one-on-one mentorships, memorization can be a helpful way to study and meditate together. For new Christians, this might be their first introduction to the concept—and a great chance to learn to think biblically. And for those trying to get into the habit of regular Bible reading, memorizing with a mentor can be a hook back into Scripture.

## Kids' Groups

### CHILDREN'S CHURCH

Whether or not the entire church is working on memorization, it's often part of the children's curriculum. Considering that most kids attend classes during services, this is a key opportunity to share the story of the Bible and explain what Jesus has done for them.

Children have a natural love for familiarity and repeated routines, so memorization is a joy rather than a challenge to be overcome. This is apparent in oft-repeated nursery rhymes, the desire to have the same bedtime stories read again and again, and the need to have the same schedules followed day after day.

Children need a lesson that ties together the story or teaching, the memorization verse, and a craft activity. Even if children are memorizing a longer verse for an entire month, it should still relate to the overall unit. Here are some ideas that can be varied for each age range:

- Speak aloud a verse word-for-word, with children repeating each word—week after week if needed!

- Use visual aids such as flannel boards or illustrated whiteboards.

- Set the verse to music, teaching it like a song.

- Add hand motions to go with each word.

- Create take-home printables so parents can help kids practice reciting during the week.

Children who are able to read and write can practice writing out verses in a variety of ways. Simple copywork on paper is one option. Many kids also love adding in crafts. Here are some fun ideas that combine the written verse with a hands-on activity:

- Write the verse on a Popsicle-stick house.

- Decorate written versions of the verse using items such as glued-on cotton balls, glitter, construction paper, and crayons.

- Attach the written verse to a take-home gift for Mom and Dad, such as an ornament or a colorful rock.

Reciting the selected verse at children's church each week is a fun activity that kids can look forward to. This is especially true when there is a potential prize at the end! Kids find great pride and joy in a job well done. Consider a few of these tried-and-true methods of motivation:

- Track successful verse memorization with sticker charts.

- Purchase small, church-themed prizes online or at your local Christian store.

- Award prizes that display the verse, such as printed bookmarks.

## YOUTH GROUP

Middle school and high school students might enjoy the challenge of working on a longer section of Scripture, such as a chapter. If meetings are consistent, perhaps even a short book of the Bible could be memorized over the course of a year. Especially in a youth group setting, activity games can be used to help memorize Scripture. This method targets the kinesthetic learning style *and* burns some energy! Here are a few options:

- **Ball Toss**—Whoever catches the ball gets to say the next word or the next sentence in the passage.

- **"Buzz-In"**—The host displays a Scripture reference, and the first team member to "buzz in" (by raising a hand, ringing a bell, or using a buzzer purchased at a game store) gets to recite it. If successful, their team gets a point. If not, the other team gets to try. The number of rounds will reflect the number of Scripture passages the group has been learning.

- **Musical Chairs**—Chairs are set up for the number of participants, minus one. A musical recording plays while participants walk single file around the lineup of chairs. At a random moment, the music is stopped, and participants scramble to find a chair. The person left standing has a chance to recite a Scripture passage to get back into the game. If they are unsuccessful, a chair is removed, and play continues until the only remaining player is declared the winner.

- **Field Trips**—Looking forward to a fun outing can encourage teens toward their memorization goals. If your group has a sufficient budget, consider a trip to the local theme park or state fair. Events like these can especially attract teens who aren't from a churched background.

Keep in mind, however, that at this age, external rewards shouldn't be the only motivator. Devotional and study elements are also important, so consider including a Bible study resource in your memorization program. You can also customize a plan that works well with the lessons you've chosen for your group.

## HOMESCHOOL BIBLE LESSONS

Many homeschoolers today have found great value in including all types of memorization in their curriculum. After all, memorization has given humanity the words it needs to express important ideas and truths, whether through nursery rhymes, poetry, or Bible verses. And for homeschoolers, the opportunities for Scripture memorization are endless!

**Charlotte Mason Method:** Young children who use the Charlotte Mason method will already be familiar with memorization. Besides Scripture, this method emphasizes memorizing poems and enjoyable sections of literature. Paraphrasing what has been taught is also a staple of this method. Although memorization requires word-for-word repetition versus rephrasing, the same skills are used. Older students also use copywork to practice handwriting skills, allowing them to focus on the content they are writing. This is ideal for memorizing Scripture verse by verse or chapter by chapter.

**Classical Method:** Young children who use the classical style start engaging in memorization during their grammar years. We already know that young children are natural imitators, a phase that classical homeschool educators call the "poll-parrot" stage. It is characterized by observation, memorization, and repetition—crucial steps as children receive straight instruction of basic facts. Memorization provides a rich vocabulary and stores of knowledge that will contribute to critical-thinking skills in the future. For older students in the "logic" and "rhetoric" stages, Scripture memorization fits right in as they memorize Greek and Latin verbs, poems, and other pieces of literature.

All homeschoolers can benefit from handwriting curricula that offers Scripture-based lessons. Creating companion memory plans means you have an easy, premade lesson with worksheets. Additionally, many homeschool Bible curricula also include verses to memorize. This is a logical choice for some parents, while others may favor verses that match what their church or family is learning.

Another alternative is to springboard off personal devotions. To check progress, schedule recitations at the end of each week. Similar to the point of many creative-writing or journaling assignments, effort is what counts rather than perfection or a grade. We want children to memorize with a joyful desire to draw closer to the Lord, not with fear of failure or judgment.

### *Family Devotions*

For many families, regular devotional time helps them spend intentional time with the Lord. As already discussed, children are natural imitators who need to see Mom and Dad spending time in prayer, discussing a Bible passage, and reciting Scripture from memory. Modeling faithfulness is important when a parent's most fervent prayer is that their children will hold to the faith. Here are a few more Scripture passages that address this topic:

## GETTING STARTED

*"My child, listen when your father corrects you. Don't neglect your mother's instruction. What you learn from them will crown you with grace and be a chain of honor around your neck."* (Prov. 1:8–9 NLT)

*"Discipline your children, and they will give you peace of mind and will make your heart glad."* (Prov. 29:17 NLT)

*"Do not provoke your children to anger, but bring them up in the discipline and instruction of the Lord."* (Eph. 6:4 ESV)

*"You must continue in the things which you have learned and been assured of, knowing from whom you have learned them, and that from childhood you have known the Holy Scriptures, which are able to make you wise for salvation through faith which is in Christ Jesus."* (2 Tim. 3:14–15 NKJV)

Devotional enthusiasm comes and goes for everyone. But when parents stay consistent with family devotions over the years, children learn the importance of choosing to draw near to the Lord, even when the desire is weak. Methods differ among families, and not all will find that a formal devotion time works. Many parents decide to take each moment as it comes. These teachable moments can also include verse instruction that helps children apply Scripture to current or future situations. And of course, such off-the-cuff instruction is most effective when parents have already memorized Scripture themselves. They can also draw from these verses when faced with the rapid-fire questions that toddlers (and teens!) often ask.

Family devotional times provide a safe place for discussing important matters like repentance and forgiveness, as well as smaller matters like "messing up" a recited Scripture passage. By placing memorization alongside Bible reading, hymn-singing, and prayer time, everyone feels less pressure. Choosing a passage to memorize requires thoughtful consideration of all members. Some families prefer a length that fits the youngest child's ability level. Others might want to customize the same passage: Adults and older children memorize the entire section, middle children memorize a little less, and young children memorize a short snippet. In this way everyone feels challenged, yet everyone remains focused on the same verses.

# TWENTY MEMORIZATION STRATEGIES

## 1. Remember Your Motivation

We already know that memorization works best as part of worship and study and that you're more likely to reach goals you find meaningful. It's helpful to keep in mind that the end result is not the same as the end goal. For example, you don't brush your teeth for the sake of brushing but rather for your dental health and hygiene. In the same way, remember to memorize not for the sake of memorization but for what it will bring to your spiritual life.

*I want to memorize Scripture because:*

_____

_____

_____

## 2. Set Realistic Goals

Speaking of goals, there's nothing quite so demotivating as failing to reach them. No one likes to diet all week and find they have gained a pound. Or say you decide to stop overspending, only to order takeout because you're too tired to cook (we've all done it!). You feel guilty for days. But when it comes to Scripture memorization, you can take heart knowing there's no pressure. Proceed at your own pace and accept interruptions as they come. If you find memorizing is harder than you anticipated, slow down and work on just a few words at a time. Setting realistic goals helps keep you motivated. Each little "win" can propel you forward to the next level. The familiar saying is true for goals of any size: "There is only one way to eat an elephant—one bite at a time."

*My realistic goal is to:*

___

___

___

## 3. Establish a Schedule

One of the main challenges we face in today's society is that we're busier than ever. Do you deal with deadline pressures and hundreds of emails every day? Maybe you work two jobs just to make ends meet. Perhaps you're a stay-at-home mom with scarcely a minute to eat. For many of us, finding time to memorize Scripture will require a simple but intentional shift. For example, try practicing a few verses during your break time at work. It's possible, however, that you may need to find additional solutions to avoid overextending yourself. One option is to ask a family member to help with childcare or household duties so you can memorize when your mind is still fresh. Just remember the main point: It's hard to accomplish anything without establishing a schedule. Simply having good intentions without practically working toward a goal is defeating to even the most motivated person.

*I will open up time to memorize Scripture by:*

## 4. Aim for Consistent Habits

You may have heard that it takes twenty-one days to form a habit and ninety days to make a lifestyle change. Yet you have probably experienced the rut of the New Year's resolution—only to fall flat by the beginning of February. How can you successfully achieve the hard work of memorizing Scripture? Creating triggers to kick off your new habit is one way. James Clear, author of the book *Atomic Habits*, talks about cues, which come in several forms. How might the following cues work for you as you seek to memorize Scripture?

- Time (such as morning or at lunch)
- Location (such as in your den or in your car while driving to work)
- Preceding event (such as a phone alarm)
- Other people (accountability partners or other family members)

*My cues are:*

_____

_____

_____

## 5. Find a Quiet Place

Research has shown that tasks involving problem solving and memory recall are performed better in silence. All noise can distract you from your task, and random background noise has proven to be the worst distraction. If you happen to find yourself stuck in a loud spot, however, there is one source of noise that may actually help you focus: music. Anything quiet, acoustic, and rhythmic works best for memory work. As you make progress, noisy interruptions can even be used as a test. If you can recall your verses in a roomful of children or with a dog barking outside, you should be able to recall them anywhere!

*My quiet place is:*

_____

_____

_____

## 6. Use Flash Cards

Flash cards are a staple for nearly anyone who is practicing memorization—foreign language learners, medical students, college students, and Bible-memory learners. You may opt to purchase flash cards that are part of a Scripture-memory system, or you can write your own verses on something as simple as index cards. This allows you to keep track of your Scripture-writing copywork, writing the verse on one side and the reference on the other. Either way, you can strew them across the house to test your ability throughout the day. They also provide a convenient way to memorize when you are out and about.

*My timeline for creating or purchasing flash cards is:*

___

___

___

## 7. Memorize Precisely

One of the primary goals of memorization is to recall the exact wording of a passage. Many of us can explain a Scripture's general meaning, but we often flounder when sharing it with others. Have you ever said, "You know, the verse that says something like …"? Statements like these don't have quite the same impact as exact words. And if you're not recalling the exact words of a passage, you might not even understand its meaning correctly. Plus, once you get a different version in your head, it's harder to even remember which one is right. Most of us have kept singing incorrect song lyrics simply because we misunderstood them in the first place. Decades later, we may know the right words, but the old ones have just stuck.

One helpful way to make sure you are memorizing precisely is to constantly recheck your work. For example, if you're using a flash card, flip it over right away once you've recited your verse. Then you can see where you might be misremembering a word. Or ask a friend or family member to listen to you recite the verse. Many actors learn their lines by working with friends who will listen and correct them—or even feed them the start of the line.

*My strategy for memorizing precisely is:*

_____

_____

## 8. Know Your Learning Style

Every person learns differently. In fact, many teachers adapt their lessons to fit a variety of learning styles. Four well-known styles include:

1. Visual

2. Auditory

3. Kinesthetic (Motion)

4. Reading/Writing

Learning in one's preferred style has been shown to increase levels of understanding. Students can still learn using methods that are outside of their preference, but they may need to put in extra effort. For example, a student who has an auditory learning style might struggle to learn from a textbook versus a spoken lesson. The reverse would be true with a student who has a reading/writing preference. However, everyone can still benefit from using a variety of methods so that the brain has multiple ways to recall information. As you read the following learning-style descriptions, think about which one fits you best.

### *Visual*

Visual learners think in pictures. For memorization, it's helpful to draw pictures or a map linking words to pictures. These serve as visual "hinges" to hang memorized words upon. For example, for "God is love" (1 John 4:8 NIV), a visual learner might draw a cross and a heart.

> *God is love.*
> 1 JOHN 4:8 NIV

For longer verses, visual learners can use acrostic-like clues to stay on track. For example, "DNQTS: '**D**o **n**ot **q**uench **t**he **s**pirit.' (1 Thess. 5:19 NIV)." Or they can create a map using key symbols to connect the words in a verse. For an example, see the word map for Matthew 4:4 on the next page.

## Auditory

Auditory learners will benefit both from reading Scripture out loud and listening to someone else read. This is a great way to learn alongside others in your family, with one reading and one listening. Another option is to memorize using an audio Bible. Many Bible apps also include an audio element. You can also record yourself repeating the same passage again and again.

## Kinesthetic (Motion)

If you like to learn kinesthetically, motion is your friend! Research shows that movement-based learning can improve memory recall, focus, and other skills. There are many ways to include motion as you memorize Scripture.

# WORD MAP FOR MATTHEW 4:4

Jesus answered,

↓

"It is written:

↓

'Man shall not live

↓

on bread alone,

↓

but on every word that comes

↓

from the mouth

↓

of God.'"

MATT. 4:4 NIV

For example, some people like to use flash cards while they walk on a treadmill at the gym. Others read or recite while pacing the room. Even a little back-and-forth sway while standing still or sitting in a chair can help. Kneading or spinning sensory toys in your hand while memorizing creates a rhythmic, monotonous movement. For little kids, silly games are often appropriate.

## *Reading/Writing*

For those with a reading/writing learning style, continually seeing and reading the passage on the page goes a long way toward remembrance. Reading a passage aloud can also help. Writing out the passage by hand before you recite it goes a long way toward achieving memorization goals. This can be done anywhere at anytime by keeping a small notebook and pen handy. Combining writing and movement is another option, such as writing out short verses in the sand or using modeling clay. Consider these benefits of writing out memory verses:

- You can check for errors by quickly comparing your work with the text in your Bible or on your flash card.

- You can significantly improve your memory work more than if you typed out the passage. Sensory connections that come with writing by hand are likely the reason. Another theory is that electronic devices bring more distractions.

## Scripture Memory and Learning Styles

| STYLE | DESCRIPTION |
|---|---|
| **Visual** | • Short verses: Draw a picture that sums up the verse.<br>• Longer verses: Create a "map" linking each word or phrase to a representative picture. |
| **Auditory** | • Read Scripture out loud.<br>• Listen to someone else read (e.g., audio Bible). |
| **Kinesthetic (Motion)** | • Combine memorization with motion.<br>• Walk, use sensory toys, or play action-oriented games. |
| **Reading/ Writing** | • Read the passage repeatedly, either silently or out loud.<br>• Write the passage longhand using pen and paper or combining with kinesthetic options such as clay. |

*My learning style is:*

_____

_____

_____

## 9. Link Words to Concepts

Linking the words of a passage to different themes or concepts is another way to memorize. Our brains are already wired to create links between people or events that are linked to the same time or place. For Scripture memorization, simply think of the visual form of a word in the passage. Visual learners may enjoy drawing the images, but any type of learner can link words with concepts in their minds. For example, for "Behold, I will extend peace to her like a river, and the glory of the nations like an overflowing stream" (Isaiah 66:12 (ESV)), you might imagine the following connections:

- A speaker ("Behold")

- An expanding tape measure ("I will extend")

- A peace sign ("peace")

- A woman ("to her")

- A river ("like a river")

- A shining gold globe ("and the glory of the nations")

- A rushing high stream ("like an overflowing stream")

*A Scripture passage I want to try with this strategy is:*

_____

_____

_____

## 10. Practice "Chunking"

"Chunking" involves taking information and breaking it down into smaller categories to memorize. For example, if you want to memorize a phone number, you can break it down by the area code, the three-digit prefix, and the final four digits. For Scripture, one method is to break down a section of verses by theme or by rhythm.

### Chunking by Theme

    **Green** words = "new covenant"
    **Blue** words = "inheritance"
    **Red** words = "ransom"
    **Black** words = "first covenant"

> *Christ is the mediator of a new covenant,*
> *that those who are called may receive the*
> *promised eternal inheritance—*
> *now that he has died as a ransom to set them free from*
> **the sins committed under the first covenant.**
>
> HEB. 9:15 NIV

*A Scripture passage I want to try with this strategy is:*

_____

_____

_____

## *Chunking by Rhythm*

Scripture that is set as poetry, such as the Psalms, can be chunked rhythmically by lines or verses:

> **[17] Be good to your servant while I live,
> that I may obey your word.**
>
> **[18] Open my eyes that I may see
> wonderful things in your law.**
>
> PSALM 119:17–18 NIV

*A Scripture passage I want to try with this strategy is:*

_____

_____

_____

_____

## 11. Explore Mnemonics

To improve your memory of Scripture passages by using mnemonics (pronounced "ni-MA-niks"), think of a visual representation for the words you want to remember (such as from the linking example above). Then think of locations you frequently encounter, such as places inside or outside your house or along a route you often walk (e.g., your doorway, your mailbox, the community library, the house with the gorgeous flowers, the next house with the garden, a car that's usually parked on the street, the post office, and so on). As you keep reciting, you can associate each location with one of the words or phrases in your passage. With each location cue, you will be able to recall the words or phrases of the passage in order. Here is an example using Isaiah 66:12 again. As you leave your house and take a walk around the neighborhood, imagine these visual connections to the words in the passage:

> ***Behold, I will extend peace to her like a river, and the glory of the nations like an overflowing stream.*** (ESV)

- A speaker standing in your doorway saying "Behold!"

- Someone using a measuring tape to measure your mailbox ("I will extend")

- The community library with a peace sign painted on the side ("peace")

- A woman tending her garden at the house with the flowers ("to her")

- A river flowing behind the house with the garden ("like a river")

- A shining gold globe hanging from the car's rearview mirror ("and the glory of the nations")

- A stamp at the post office that features an overflowing river ("like an overflowing stream")

*A Scripture passage I want to try with this strategy is:*

___

___

___

## 12. Repeat Often

Probably starting with the ancient Romans, the phrase "Repetition is the mother of learning" has been a motto for centuries—and for good reason! Repetition leads to mastery of a subject at a much higher level, moving information from short-term memory to long-term memory. It keeps words fresh in our minds and prevents those pesky mistakes that want to stay with us. Repetition motivates us with the assurance that we will achieve higher accuracy than we would by making random, spread-apart attempts at Scripture memory.

*A Scripture passage I want to try with this strategy is:*

_____

_____

_____

## 13. Keep It in Front of You

Keeping Scripture in front of you during the day is another way to give yourself a nudge to memorize. Place your flash cards or sticky notes with verses written them in spots where your eyes often fall. Some examples include your bathroom mirror, inside the fridge, and on a door. Each time you see the note is another chance to practice reading the passage and saying it out loud. This helps you improve accuracy and get those reps in!

*Places where I can post Scriptures include:*

_____

_____

_____

## 14. Set Scripture to Music

Besides helping with focus amid a noisy setting, music can benefit memorization in other ways. Music helps improve memory, reasoning, and speech, plus it helps us recall old memories and make new memories. One doesn't have to be an instrumentalist or a singer for music to help with memorization. Scripture-memory music is available for purchase, but there's also nothing wrong with simply making up a melody to go with your Scripture verse. You can also set the passage to a well-known tune.

*A Scripture passage I want to try with this strategy is:*

_____

_____

## 15. Share Your Passage

It's often said that we don't really know something until we can explain it to others. Sharing the Scripture you've memorized allows you to share God's truth with others and practice your recitation at the same time. It's a great opportunity to help others understand Scripture or share how it has impacted your life. Plus, sharing in a social setting, where there are lots of distractions, will strengthen your memorization skills!

*A Scripture passage and social setting I want to try with this strategy is:*

_____

_____

## 16. Review Regularly

It's quite annoying to work hard memorizing a passage, only to move on to the next one and realize you've forgotten the previous one! Unfortunately, the brain is all too efficient at removing information it thinks isn't necessary anymore. Regular review keeps your memory fresh and tells the brain what is worth keeping around. It also provides a chance to touch up what is rusty—sticky words, close-but-not-quite-correct phrasing, mixed-up verses within chapters, and any other slight alterations from the text you're memorizing. Consider spacing out your memory work by having regular review sessions between each new memory verse.

*Some ways I can review regularly include:*

_____

_____

_____

## 17. Take Quizzes

Many of us don't have fond memories of taking quizzes, but they are a time-honored method for reviewing your work. Sitting down for a quiz may help you realize you don't actually know the passage as well as you thought! Thankfully, Scripture memorization doesn't require a "pop quiz" element. Simple quizzing brings effective results.

It provides a reality check to ensure you're not just going merrily along the way with errors. After all, reciting a few words and looking back at the passage can easily become a habit. The result is that you are not committing the passage to long-term memory. You can have someone quiz you verbally, or simply record yourself reciting the passage and then check your work afterward. You can also quiz yourself using flash cards. Mix them randomly to test whether you are relying on familiar patterns or genuinely recalling the words and matching them with the correct reference.

*My methods for taking quizzes can include:*

---

---

---

## 18. Overcome Ruts

Let's say you're successful at memorizing a few passages, but then the momentum stops. Maybe you're too overwhelmed by everything that is going on in your life. Or maybe you're simply procrastinating. What do you do when the motivation just won't come? Perhaps the most helpful solution is to return to your core goal of spending time with the Lord. It's okay if you need to simply read your Bible and spend time in God's presence for a while. There's no law that says you must be memorizing Scripture at every moment. If you release yourself from expectations, sometimes the desire will return after the pressure goes away. Instead of focusing your attention on the process, focus on the Lord and serving him.

Also, take time to examine your goals. Were you a little too ambitious? If so, think about how to scale back. Accept that there will always be delays and interruptions. If you're dealing with procrastination or boredom—or if the thrill of a new challenge has faded—restarting can often be very hard. Dive back in with verses you're already familiar with. The sooner you restart, the sooner a feeling of accomplishment will follow. Giving yourself a small reward can help. For example, tell yourself, *I'll practice my memory work first, and then I'll get my coffee.* Sometimes strategies like these are enough to get you back in the game and looking forward to making progress.

*Some rewards that will help me continue memorizing are:*

_____

_____

_____

## 19. Pray Often

Jesus said, "Ask, and it will be given to you; seek, and you will find; knock, and it will be opened to you" (Matt. 7:7 ESV). The Lord does not turn a deaf ear to those seeking to know him better and understand his Word more. Ask him to bless your efforts to hide Scripture in your heart. Ask him to help you call it to mind as you go about daily life. He is faithful to answer!

*My prayer is:*

___

___

___

___

## 20. Remember the Bottom Line

Whether you memorize on your own or with a group, using whichever methods work best for you, know that God will bless your efforts. It may not always be easy, but the rewards of drawing near to him will last a lifetime. Romans 2:6–7 sums it up well:

> **[God] will give eternal life to those who keep on doing good, seeking after the glory and honor and immortality that God offers.** (NLT)

*I'm looking forward to these rewards of Scripture memorization:*

_____

_____

_____

_____

# SCRIPTURES TO MEMORIZE

## Ten Key Passages to Memorize

*God so loved the world that he gave his one and only Son, that whoever believes in him shall not perish but have eternal life.*

JOHN 3:16 NIV

---

*If we confess our sins, he is faithful and just and will forgive us our sins and purify us from all unrighteousness.*

1 JOHN 1:9 NIV

---

*It is by grace you have been saved, through faith— and this is not from yourselves, it is the gift of God— not by works, so that no one can boast.*

EPHESIANS 2:8–9 NIV

---

*Trust in the LORD with all your heart and lean not on your own understanding; in all your ways submit to him, and he will make your paths straight.*

PROVERBS 3:5–6 NIV

*Do not conform to the pattern of this world, but be transformed by the renewing of your mind. Then you will be able to test and approve what God's will is—his good, pleasing and perfect will.*

ROMANS 12:2 NIV

---

*The fruit of the Spirit is love, joy, peace, forbearance, kindness, goodness, faithfulness, gentleness and self-control. Against such things there is no law.*

GALATIANS 5:22–23 NIV

---

*Let your light shine before others, that they may see your good deeds and glorify your Father in heaven.*

MATTHEW 5:16 NIV

---

*Whatever were gains to me I now consider loss for the sake of Christ. What is more, I consider everything a loss because of the surpassing worth of knowing Christ Jesus my Lord.*

PHILIPPIANS 3:7–8 NIV

**SCRIPTURES TO MEMORIZE**

*Do not be anxious about anything,
but in every situation, by prayer and petition,
with thanksgiving, present your requests to God.*

PHILIPPIANS 4:6 NIV

---

*Rejoice always, pray continually,
give thanks in all circumstances;
for this is God's will for you in Christ Jesus.*

1 THESSALONIANS 5:16–18 NIV

## Eight Longer Passages to Memorize

1. *Matthew 6:9–15*
   **The Lord's Prayer**

2. *Psalm 23:1–6*
   **"The Lord Is My Shepherd"**

3. *Matthew 5:2–12*
   **The Beatitudes**

4. *Ephesians 6:10–20*
   **The Armor of God**

5. *1 Corinthians 13:1–13*
   **The Love Chapter**

6. *Exodus 20:1–17*
   **The Ten Commandments**

7. *Psalm 103*
   **A Psalm of David**

8. *Colossians 3:1–17*
   **Made Alive in Christ**

# Key Memory Verses: Books of the Bible

## OLD TESTAMENT

Genesis 17:3–7
Exodus 3:14
Leviticus 20:7–8
Numbers 6:24–26
Deuteronomy 6:4–5
Joshua 1:7
Judges 21:25
Ruth 1:16
1 Samuel 15:22
2 Samuel 7:8–9
1 Kings 3:9
2 Kings 19:15
1 Chronicles 4:10
2 Chronicles 7:14
Ezra 3:11
Nehemiah 8:10
Esther 4:14
Job 19:25–26
Psalm 145:21
Proverbs 3:5–6
Ecclesiastes 12:13–14
Song of Songs/
Song of Solomon 8:7
Isaiah 9:6
Jeremiah 29:11
Lamentations 3:22–23
Ezekiel 36:26
Daniel 2:44
Hosea 4:6
Joel 2:28
Amos 5:14
Obadiah 1:10
Jonah 4:2
Micah 6:8
Nahum 1:7
Habakkuk 3:18
Zephaniah 1:14
Haggai 2:5
Zechariah 9:9
Malachi 4:2

## NEW TESTAMENT

Matthew 28:18–19
Mark 10:43–45
Luke 9:23–24
John 3:16
Acts 1:8
Romans 12:1–2
1 Corinthians 13:4–5
2 Corinthians 12:9
Galatians 5:22–23
Ephesians 2:8–9
Philippians 2:14–15
Colossians 2:9–10
1 Thessalonians 5:16–22
2 Thessalonians 3:4–6
1 Timothy 4:12–13
2 Timothy 3:15–17
Titus 3:4–7
Philemon 17–19
Hebrews 12:2
James 1:19–20
1 Peter 4:7
2 Peter 1:21
1 John 4:8
2 John 1:8
3 John 1:4
Jude 1:24–25
Revelation 21:1

# Key Memory Verses about Jesus

## *Life of Jesus*

**Birth in Bethlehem**
Matthew 1:18–25; Luke 2:1–20

**Childhood**
Matthew 2:1–23; Luke 2:21–52

**Baptized**
Matthew 3:13–17; Mark 1:9–11;
Luke 3:21–22; John 1:29–34

**Tempted in the Wilderness**
Matthew 4:1–11; Mark 1:12–13;
Luke 4:1–13

**Changes Water into Wine**
John 2:1–11

**Speaks with Nicodemus**
John 3:1–21

**Speaks with the Samaritan Woman**
John 4:4–26

**Heals a Man with Leprosy**
Matthew 8:1–4; Mark 1:40–45;
Luke 5:12–14

**Heals a Paralyzed Man**
Matthew 9:1–8; Mark 2:1–12;
Luke 5:17–26

**Heals the Centurion's Servant**
Matthew 8:5–13; Luke 7:1–10

**Raises a Widow's Son from the Dead**
Luke 7:11–17

**Anointed by a Forgiven Woman**
Luke 7:36–50

**Calms the Storm**
Matthew 8:23–27; Mark 4:35–41;
Luke 8:22–25

**Casts Out Demons**
Matthew 8:28–34; Mark 5:1–20;
Luke 8:26–39

**Heals the Woman Who Touched His Cloak**
Matthew 9:20–22; Mark 5:25–34;
Luke 8:43–48

**Feeds the Crowd of 5,000**
Matthew 14:13–21; Mark 6:32–44;
Luke 9:10–17; John 6:1–13

**Walks on Water**
Matthew 14:22–33; Mark 6:45–51;
John 6:16–21

**Peter's Confession of Christ**
Matthew 16:13–20; Mark 8:27–30;
Luke 9:18–22

**Transfiguration**
Matthew 17:1–8; Mark 9:2–8;
Luke 9:28–36

**SCRIPTURES TO MEMORIZE**

**Forgives the Woman Caught in Adultery**
John 8:2–11

**Visits with Mary and Martha**
Luke 10:38–42

**Heals a Man Born Blind**
John 9:1–7

**Raises Lazarus from the Dead**
John 11:1–44

**Heals Ten People with Leprosy**
Luke 17:11–19

**Speaks with the Rich Young Man**
Matthew 19:16–30; Mark 10:17–31; Luke 18:18–30

**Zacchaeus the Tax Collector**
Luke 19:1–10

**Palm Sunday**
Matthew 21:1-11; Mark 11:1-10; Luke 19:28-38; John 12:12-15

**Clears the Temple**
Matthew 21:12-13; Mark 11:15-17; Luke 19:45-46

**The Last Supper**
Matthew 26:17-30; Mark 14:12-26; Luke 22:7-38; John 13:1-30

**In the Garden of Gethsemane**
Matthew 26:36–56; Mark 14:32–50; Luke 22:39–53; John 18:1–11

**Suffers and Dies on the Cross**
Matthew 27:26–50; Mark 15:16–37; Luke 22:63–23:46; John 19:1–30

**Resurrection and Ascension**
Matthew 28:1–20; Mark 16:1–19; Luke 24:1–53; John 20:1–18

## *Teachings and Parables of Jesus*

**Beatitudes/Sermon on the Mount**
Matthew 5:1–7:29

**Golden Rule**
Matthew 7:12; Luke 6:31

**Good Samaritan**
Luke 10:25–37

**Great Commission**
Matthew 28:18–20; Mark 16:15–16

**Greatest Commandment**
Matthew 22:34–40; Mark 12:28–34

**Hidden Treasure/Valuable Pearl**
Matthew 13:44–46

**Lord's Prayer**
Matthew 6:9–13; Luke 11:1–4

**Lost Sheep**
Matthew 18:10–14; Luke 15:1–7

**Mustard Seed**
Matthew 13:31–32; Mark 4:30–32;
Luke 13:18–19

**Pearl of Great Price**
Matthew 13:45–46

**Persistent Widow**
Luke 18:2–8

**Prodigal Son**
Luke 15:11–32

**Rich Man and Lazarus**
Luke 16:19–31

**Sheep and Goats**
Matthew 25:31–46

**Shrewd Manager**
Luke 16:1–13

**Sower and the Seeds**
Matthew 13:1–23; Mark 4:1–20;
Luke 8:4–15

**Talents**
Matthew 25:14–30; Luke 19:12–27

**Ten Virgins**
Matthew 25:1–13

**Unmerciful Servant**
Matthew 18:21–35

## *Savior*
Luke 19:10
John 1:1–14
John 10:10
John 11:25–26
John 14:6
Acts 4:12

## *Loving Lord and Teacher*
John 8:31–32
John 13:13–15
Ephesians 3:18
Philippians 2:10–11

## *Coming Again in Glory*
Mark 13:26
John 14:2–3
Acts 1:11

# Key Memory Verses by Topic

## Angels
Psalm 91:11
Matthew 18:10

## Armor of God
Ephesians 6:10–20

## Baptism
Mark 1:8
Romans 6:4

## Bible
Psalm 119:11
Psalm 119:105
Isaiah 55:11
2 Timothy 3:16
Hebrews 4:12

## Childlessness
Isaiah 54:1–3

## Children
Matthew 18:3
Matthew 18:6
Matthew 19:14
Ephesians 6:1

## Church
Matthew 16:18
Hebrews 10:25

## Discipleship
Joshua 24:15
Ruth 1:16
1 Samuel 2:30
1 Samuel 15:22
Matthew 6:33
Matthew 10:32–33
Mark 8:35
Luke 9:23
John 14:23
Galatians 2:20
Philippians 1:21

## Encouragement

**When You're Afraid**
Joshua 1:5
Esther 4:14
Psalm 20:7
Psalm 23:4
Psalm 27:1
Psalm 56:11
Proverbs 24:19–20
Isaiah 41:13
Isaiah 43:1
Zephaniah 3:17
Matthew 10:28
Romans 8:31

**When You're Angry**
Proverbs 15:1
Ephesians 4:26
James 1:19
1 Peter 3:9

**When You're Confused**
Psalm 37:23–24
Prov. 3:5–6
Isaiah 43:19
Jeremiah 29:11
Romans 8:28
James 1:5

**When You're Depressed**
Numbers 6:24–26
Nehemiah 8:10
Psalm 42:1–2
Psalm 147:3
Isaiah 61:1
Lamentations 3:22–23
John 16:33
Philippians 4:8–9

**When You're Doubting Your Salvation**
Psalm 103:12
John 5:24
John 6:47
John 10:28
Philippians 1:6

**When You're Envious**
Psalm 37:4
Proverbs 30:8–9
Philippians 4:11
Hebrews 13:5

**When You're Grieving**
Isaiah 25:8
Matthew 5:4
1 Corinthians 15:54-57
2 Corinthians 5:6
1 Thessalonians 4:13–18

**When You're Harmed**
Genesis 50:20
Proverbs 25:21
Matthew 5:10–12
Matthew 5:23–24
Matthew 6:14
Luke 17:3–4

**When You're Impatient**
Psalm 27:14
Psalm 40:1–2
Ecclesiastes 3:1–11
Ephesians 4:2
Colossians 3:12
2 Timothy 2:22–23

**When You're Lonely**
Psalm 107:9
Psalm 139:1–10
Matthew 28:20
John 16:32
Romans 8:39

**When You're Regretting Sin**
2 Chronicles 7:14
Psalm 51:10–12
Psalm 103:8
James 4:8
1 John 1:9

## SCRIPTURES TO MEMORIZE

**When You're Sick**
2 Corinthians 4:16–18
James 5:6
James 5:14–15

**When You're Suffering**
Job 19:25–27
Psalm 18:2
Psalm 34:6
Psalm 121:1–2
Isaiah 30:18–19
Isaiah 41:10
2 Corinthians 4:7–9
1 Peter 1:6–7

**When You're Tempted**
Matthew 6:13
Matthew 26:41
Luke 22:40
1 Corinthians 10:13
Hebrews 2:18
James 1:13–15
James 4:7

**When You're Tired**
Isaiah 12:2
Isaiah 40:28–31
Matthew 11:28–30
2 Corinthians 12:9
Philippians 4:13
2 Timothy 4:7
Hebrews 6:10–12
Hebrews 12:1–3
James 1:2–4

**When You're Worried**
Proverbs 3:5–6
Jeremiah 17:7–8
Zechariah 4:6
Matthew 6:34
Philippians 4:6–7
Philippians 4:19
1 Peter 5:7

*End Times*
Matthew 24:6
Matthew 24:42
1 Thessalonians 4:17
1 Thessalonians 5:2
2 Peter 3:8–10

*Faith*
Matthew 17:20
Romans 10:17
Hebrews 11:1
Hebrews 11:6

*False Teachers*
Matthew 7:15
Galatians 1:8

*Friendship*
Proverbs 17:17
Proverbs 27:17
Ecclesiastes 4:12

*Fruit of the Spirit*
Galatians 5:22–23

## Giving
Proverbs 11: 24–25
Malachi 3:10
2 Corinthians 9:7

## God

### Almighty Lord
Psalm 48:1
Psalm 147:4–5
Isaiah 55:8–9
Luke 1:37

### Loving Creator
Psalm 8:4–5
Psalm 100:3
Psalm 139:13–16
Luke 12:6–7

### The Only God
Deuteronomy 6:4
Isaiah 44:6
Isaiah 45:5
Matthew 4:10

## Good Works
Matthew 25:40
Romans 12:20-21
Galatians 6:7–11
Ephesians 2:10
Philippians 2:4
James 1:22
James 1:27
James 2:17

## Gospel

### Believing in Jesus
John 11:25
Acts 2:21
Romans 10:9
Ephesians 2:8–9
1 John 1:9
Revelation 3:20

### Called to Share
Isaiah 52:7
Matthew 5:14–16
Romans 1:16
Colossians 4:5–6
2 Timothy 1:7
2 Timothy 1:12
2 Timothy 4:2
1 Peter 3:15

### Jesus's Sacrifice for Us
Isaiah 53:3–5
John 3:16–18
Romans 3:25
Romans 5:8
1 Corinthians 15:3–4
Colossians 1:19–20

### Our New Life
Isaiah 1:18
Romans 8:1–2
Titus 3:4–7
1 John 5:11–12

# SCRIPTURES TO MEMORIZE

**Sin and Its Consequences**
Jeremiah 17:9
Romans 3:23
Romans 5:12
Romans 6:23

## Gossip
Psalm 34:12–13
Proverbs 11:13
Proverbs 17:9
Ephesians 4:29

## Government
Luke 20:25
Acts 5:28–29
Titus 3:1
Heaven
Isaiah 11:6
Isaiah 51:11
John 14:1–3
1 Corinthians 13:10–13
2 Corinthians 5:8
Philippians 3:20
1 John 3:2
Revelation 21:4
Revelation 22:4

## Holy Spirit

**His Empowerment**
Acts 1:8
Acts 2:4
1 Corinthians 12:4–13
Ephesians 3:16

**His Guidance**
John 14:16
John 14:26
John 16:13

**His Presence with Us**
Romans 8:26
1 Corinthians 6:19
Galatians 4:6
Ephesians 1:13–14

## Humility and Pride
Proverbs 16:18
Philippians 2:3
James 4:10
1 Peter 5:5-6

## Hypocrisy
1 Samuel 16:7
Isaiah 29:13
Matthew 7:1–5
Matthew 23:27

## Identity in Christ

**Accepted**
Romans 15:7

**Alive with Christ**
Ephesians 2:4–5

**Baptized into Christ**
Romans 6:3–4

**Body of Christ**
1 Corinthians 12:27

**Born Again**
John 3:3-7

**Called**
Romans 8:28–30

**Children of God**
1 John 3:1–2

**Children of Promise**
Galatians 4:28

**Chosen**
2 Thessalonians 2:13

**Citizens of Heaven**
Philippians 3:20

**Empowered by God**
Ephesians 6:10-17

**Entrusted with the Secrets of God**
1 Corinthians 4:1

**Fishers of Men**
Mark 1:17

**Forgiven**
Colossians 2:13

**Friends of Jesus**
John 15:15

**Holy**
1 Peter 1:15–16

**Instruments for Noble Purposes**
2 Timothy 2:20-21

**Lights in the World**
Matthew 5:14–16

**Loved**
1 John 4:10

**Ministers of Reconciliation**
2 Corinthians 5:18

**New Creations**
2 Corinthians 5:17

**One in Christ**
Galatians 3:28

**Purified**
1 John 1:9

**Raised with Christ**
Colossians 3:1

**Redeemed**
1 Peter 1:18–19

**Royal Priesthood**
1 Peter 2:9

**Saints**
Romans 1:7

**Saved**
Acts 16:30–31

**Servants of God**
2 Corinthians 6:4

**Soldiers of Christ**
2 Timothy 2:3

# SCRIPTURES TO MEMORIZE

**Temple of the Holy Spirit**
1 Corinthians 6:19

**Victorious**
1 Corinthians 15:57

## Justice
Leviticus 19:15
Psalm 82:3–4
Isaiah 30:18
Micah 6:8
Malachi 3:5

## Kindness and Mercy
Hosea 6:6
Luke 6:31
Colossians 3:12

## Lord's Supper
Luke 22:19
1 Corinthians 11:26

## Love
Matthew 22:37
John 13:34–35
John 15:13
1 Corinthians 13
1 Peter 4:8
1 John 3:18
1 John 4:7

## Marriage
Genesis 2:24
Proverbs 5:18–20
2 Corinthians 6:14
Ephesians 5:21–33
Hebrews 13:4
1 Peter 3:7

## Missions
Isaiah 6:8
Matthew 28:18–20
Acts 1:8
Romans 10:14
1 Corinthians 9:20–22

## Money
Deuteronomy 8:18
Job 1:21
Proverbs 3:9
Matthew 6:19–24
Matthew 19:24–26
Matthew 20:16
Mark 8:36
Luke 12:48
Luke 16:10
1 Timothy 6:10

## Parenting
Deuteronomy 6:6–9
Psalm 127:3
Proverbs 22:6
Ephesians 6:4

## Praise and Worship
Psalm 100:4
Romans 12:1
1 Corinthians 10:31
Philippians 4:4

### Prayer
Isaiah 55:6
Isaiah 65:24
Jeremiah 33:3
Matthew 7:7-11
Matthew 18:20
Ephesians 6:18
1 Thessalonians 5:17
James 5:16
1 John 5:14

### Satan
2 Corinthians 11:14
James 4:7
1 Peter 5:8–9

### Sexual Immorality
1 Corinthians 6:9–10
1 Corinthians 6:13–18
1 Thessalonians 4:3

### Singleness
1 Corinthians 7:32

### Spiritual Gifts
Romans 12:3–8
1 Corinthians 12:4–11
1 Peter 4:10

### Truthfulness
Proverbs 12:22
Matthew 5:37
Ephesians 4:25

### Unity in Christ
Psalm 133:1
John 17:20–21
Galatians 3:28
Ephesians 4:25

### Wisdom
1 Corinthians 1:18–25
Colossians 2:8
James 1:5

### Work
Matthew 25:21
Ephesians 4:28
Colossians 3:23–24

### Worldliness
John 15:18
John 17:15–16
Romans 12:2
2 Corinthians 10:3–5
1 John 2:15

# RESOURCES

## Adults

**Topical Memory System**
NavPress
9781576839973 (*Hide God's Word in Your Heart*, softcover)
9781600066719 (*Life Issues*, softcover)

**A Genesis to Revelation Scripture Memory Guide**
Ed Strauss
Barbour Books
978-1683222453 (softcover)

**Life Verse: Discovering the Power of Scripture in Your Story**
David Edwards
NavPress
9781612917757 (Kindle e-book)

**NIV Listener's Audio Bible**
Vocal Performance by Max McLean
Zondervan
Audio download, CDs

**Bible Audio App: Listen to the Bible Everywhere**
Bible Gateway/HarperCollins Christian Publishing
Google Play, Apple Store

### Bible Memory Verses: 52-Week Bible Memory Verse Flash Cards
Briston

### Integrity Music's Scripture Memory Songs
Audio downloads
Topics such as:
- Comfort
- Encouragement
- Faith
- Forgiveness
- God's promises, provision, wisdom, and will
- Grace
- Overcoming fear, guilt, and stress
- Worship

## Kids

### Topical Memory System for Kids
NavPress
Ages 5–7
9781641583343 (*Hide God's Word in Your Heart*, softcover)
9781641585507 (*Be Like Jesus!*, softcover)

### Top 50 Memory Verse Lessons with Games and Activities
Lindsey Whitney
RoseKidz
Ages 5–10
9781628625059 (softcover)

## RESOURCES

### 77 Memory Verses Every Kid Should Know
Christian Art Kids
Ages 5–8
9781432130770 (softcover)

### Visual Bible Verse Devotions: 52 Weeks of Memorizing God's Promises
Michele Howe
RoseKidz
Ages 5–10
9781628628418 (softcover)

### Go Bible Key Verse Challenge: Scripture Memory Key Verse Cards
Brock Eastman and Talia Messina
Tyndale Kids
Ages 7–11
9798400500251 (softcover with 125+ illustrated cards)

### The Biggest Story Verse Cards
Illustrated by Don Clark
Crossway Publishers
Grades K–5
60069371434871 (104 illustrated cards)

### Bible Memory Verses Every Kid Should Know
Coloring Cards
Christian Art Kids
60069371434871 (52 cards)

**Hidden in My Heart Scripture Memory Songs, vols. 1–3**
Stephen Elkins
Tyndale House/Wonder Kids
Ages 3–10
Audio downloads

**Hide 'Em in Your Heart: Bible Memory Melodies, vols. 1–2**
Steve Green
Sparrow Records
Audio downloads, CDs

# NOTES

1. For an excellent discussion of this practice, see Justin Borger, "Don't Forsake the Public Reading of Scripture," July 2020, *Tabletalk: https://tabletalkmagazine.com/posts/dont-forsake-the-public-reading-of-scripture/*.

2. Lynne Kelly, "Medieval Memories—Illuminated Manuscripts," blog, *https://www.lynnekelly.com.au/?p=277*.

3. Martin Luther: Timothy F. Lull and William R. Russell, eds., *Martin Luther's Basic Theological Writings*, 3rd ed. (Fortress, 2012), 497.

4. Jim Elliot: Nancy Flory, "'Not My Will': Jim and Elisabeth Elliot, Following God No Matter What," December 4, 2016, *The Stream: https://stream.org/not-my-will-jim-elisabeth-elliot-following-god/*.

5. Stephen W. Hines, *A Prairie Girl's Faith: The Spiritual Legacy of Laura Ingalls Wilder* (Waterbrook, 2019), 7.

6. Thomas Watson, in *Puritan Sermons*, vol. 2 (Richard Owen Roberts Publishers, 1981), 62.

7. "Overall Most Popular Bible Verses in 2022," *Bible Gateway: https://www.biblegateway.com/year-in-review/2022/*.

8. Candice Watters, "The Vast Benefits of Church-Wide Scripture Memory," January 5, 2022, *Fighter Verses: https://www.fighterverses.com/post/the-vast-benefits-of-church-wide-scripture-memory*.

# MADE EASY

## by Rose Publishing

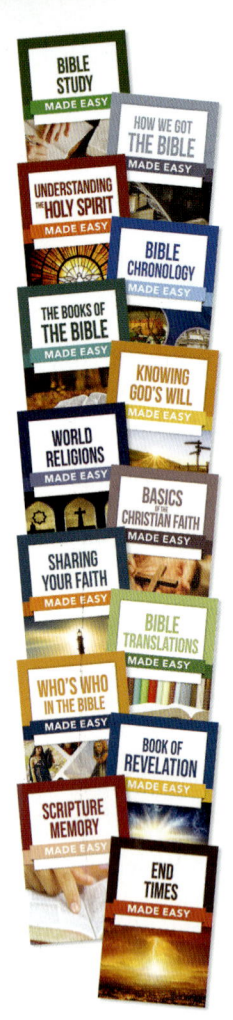

**BIBLE STUDY MADE EASY**
A step-by-step guide to studying God's Word

**HOW WE GOT THE BIBLE MADE EASY**
Key events in the history of the Bible

**UNDERSTANDING THE HOLY SPIRIT MADE EASY**
Who the Holy Spirit is and what he does

**BIBLE CHRONOLOGY MADE EASY**
Bible characters and events in the order they happened

**THE BOOKS OF THE BIBLE MADE EASY**
Quick summaries of all 66 books of the Bible

**KNOWING GOD'S WILL MADE EASY**
Answers to tough questions about God's will

**WORLD RELIGIONS MADE EASY**
30 religions and how they compare to Christianity

**BASICS OF THE CHRISTIAN FAITH MADE EASY**
Key Christian beliefs and practices

**SHARING YOUR FAITH MADE EASY**
How to share the gospel

**BIBLE TRANSLATIONS MADE EASY**
Compares 20 popular Bible versions

**BOOK OF REVELATION**
Who, what, where, when, and why of Revelation

**WHO'S WHO IN THE BIBLE**
Key facts about the Bible's main characters

**SCRIPTURE MEMORY MADE EASY**
Strategies for hiding God's Word in your heart

**END TIMES MADE EASY**
Presents key Christian views of the End Times

www.hendricksonrose.com